Little Gifts

Also by Peter Santos

Fiction

The Light Beyond the Shadows: A Tale of Awakening

Non-fiction

Everything I Wanted to Know About Spirituality but Didn't Know How to Ask: A Spiritual Seeker's Guidebook

The Little Book of Spiritual Growth: A Straightforward Primer on Energy, God, Spirit, Soul, and Ego

For children

Little Gifts: The Adventures of a Pigeon-Angel

Little Gifts

Poems to Awaken the Spirit Within

Peter Santos

Spirit Speaks Publishing
Berlin, Vermont

Little Gifts: Poems to Awaken the Spirit Within

Copyright © 2013, 2023 by Peter Santos.

All rights reserved. No part of this book may be reproduced or transmitted in any form or manner whatsoever without express written permission in writing from the publisher and copyright holder, except in the case of brief quotations embodied in critical articles and reviews. No part of this book may be used in any manner for purposes of training artificial intelligence (AI) technologies or for generative AI use without the author's express, written permission.

No generative AI was used in the creation of this book.

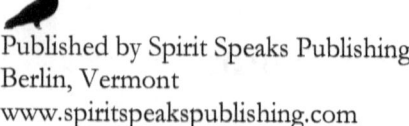

Published by Spirit Speaks Publishing
Berlin, Vermont
www.spiritspeakspublishing.com

ISBN-13: 978-1945705106

Table of Contents

Preface	ix
Introduction	xiii
MAGNIFICENCE	3
ICY REFLECTIONS	4
LITTLE GIFTS	6
COTTONBROOK	8
DJ OF THE GODS	10
BEEHIVE	12
I LET IT COME	14
EMOTIONAL WINDS	15
BATTLE OF THE OPPOSITES	16
THE MAGIC	18
PLUMBER'S WRENCH	20
A CLEVER FOE	22

IN THE STILLNESS	24
DAWN	26
YOU	29
EVERY DAY	31
MOBIUS	32
JUDAS'S GIFT	34
HAVE A GOOD TRIP	38
POINTS OF LIGHT	40
TOKEN	41
ANT	42
ENOUGH WITH WORDS	43
COMMITMENT TO TRUTH	44
THE GOD DOCTOR	46
COMMUNION	48
ETHERIC BUBBLES	51
A LITTLE ONE	52
LITTLE STRINGS	53

A THIRD TIME	54
EQUANIMITY	56
A FATHER'S THANKS	57

Preface

I never really thought of myself as a poet until I went away for a week to the Vermont Studio Center in Johnson, Vermont to spend some time writing. There I found that a distant context was informing the stories I was attempting to write, whispering layered meanings through simple phrases as the tales struggled to take form.

I have been fortunate to have travelled extensively around the world, experiencing many different countries and cultures from which to draw inspiration. Some of this travel was quite physically difficult, which often brought with it a mental and emotional exhaustion. This lent itself to the stripping away of many of the details of the personality, allowing for a detached insight into myself that I likely would not have had if not for being in a far-off land and struggling to put one foot in front of the other. There is a wonderful sense of peace that can come through the meditative sounds of labored breathing and the repetitive crunch-crunch of footsteps on a path.

I uncovered much about myself during these times: what is truly important, where my boundaries lie, who is underneath the person defined with an occupational label. These and other insights helped me come closer to understanding how I processed the world around me and how my motivating rationalizations were shrewdly undermining where I really wanted to go and what I really wanted to do.

Beyond those realizations, however, was something that had an even greater impact on me, a feeling difficult to describe. A *feeling*. It would most often come when I was physically engaged and mentally roaming, leaving fertile ground for the present moment to sneak up and pounce, which it did at times into every cell in my body. It made me feel as if nothing on earth mattered except for exactly what I was doing, and whatever that was was perfect, with no exceptions. It was a total and complete oneness with the task at hand. In those moments, I lost myself and any intentions, with no past or future to worry about, and found a peace in the moment that made all else disappear. The journey, I came to experience, was indeed more important than the destination.

It was thoughts of these feelings that came back to me as I began writing at the Vermont Studio Center. What emerged was a small number of poems that set the stage for additional poems many years and many experiences later. Throughout it all, my quest to further understand myself led to additional travel and extensive study of spiritual matters, culminating in major life changes and ultimately leading to the publishing of this collection.

I hope the words on these pages poke at your mind, tug at your heartstrings, make you consider living beyond the routines of your daily life, and give you the sense of the wonder that I experienced while on my travels, making the ordinary extraordinary. As it already is.

Peter Santos
July, 2013

Introduction

It has been said that we see less than one percent of the electromagnetic spectrum and hear less than one percent of the acoustic spectrum, leaving the remaining ninety-nine percent of each to the unknown. Whether true or not, it is clear that there are many things beyond our corporeal sensory perceptions. Our scientific instruments, essentially extensions of our physical senses, continue to observe and measure the natural world in ever more wondrous and refined ways, leading us to a greater understanding and appreciation of what makes the universe tick. Even some things that were once considered magic can now be clearly explained by newly discovered science. Nevertheless, despite sometimes obvious evidence, we always possess the ability to choose whether or not to accept the new information.

Opportunities to expand our awareness lie in that choice. It is often easier to hold onto long-standing entrenched paradigms than to allow new and exciting concepts that shake our foundational beliefs to enter into our reality.

Some of the ideas in this book may serve to challenge our comfortable routines and lives, which are built in part upon these archaic preconceived notions. Our feeling of security with these beliefs can frequently be inversely proportional to the resistance we feel when they are challenged. That is, the more we feel resistance to a new concept, the less secure we truly are in the belief that that concept challenges. This process mostly occurs subconsciously so we may feel the resistance as anxiety, fear, anger, prejudice, or other such negative emotions. Someone genuinely secure in their beliefs would most likely not feel so threatened.

Approaching each poem purposefully, with a healthy degree of openness to new perceptions, may help reveal a depth of meaning that may not be apparent through a quick read. Mentally stepping outside of the conscious reading mind into a place where reactions to the poems are observed rather than simply read may also provide a certain depth of personal insight.

As with much poetry and prose, there is beauty in the words, sentences, paragraphs, and themes that present themselves. As such, the written word serves, like our scientific instruments, as an extension of our senses, but it can also take us beyond the five senses and beyond what we believe is perceptible. Writing often tries to encapsulate experiences as *felt* rather than simply as described, attempting to evoke an increased awareness of ourselves and how we relate to the world around us.

The following collection will not be seen in any way as scientific, but it contains the opportunity to open and extend the senses nonetheless.

Little Gifts

MAGNIFICENCE

Your struggle
is senseless
in light
of who you are,

but only because
you think
you are someone else.

See Yourself
and the Universe
will carry you to
to Your
Magnificence.

ICY REFLECTIONS

An iceberg
composes its reflection
in the frosty waters
of the dream.

With shadowy fractures,
the discernable peak
reasons,
but the smooth colossus beneath
governs.

As one,
they create and destroy
their world.

The castles of glistening ice
echo deep with imitation,
vibrations reverberating
into their complexities.

A recognition,
caught in a mirror,
cracks the icy creation
with warmth and
simple clarity.

Inevitably,
the iceberg thaws,
the reflections diminish,
until once again
the sea consumes
the dream.

LITTLE GIFTS

A pigeon-angel once left
a little gift
on the shoulder of a man,
distracted by himself,
rushing to cross a busy street.

"Everybody else does,
why not you?!"
cried the man,
stopping
to shake his fist in the air.

Poor man.

He did not see the light
change
as he cursed his luck.

The pigeon-angel
watched the cars speed by,
smiled, and flew away,
looking to give away
more little gifts.

COTTONBROOK

I run
through the tall grasses
along the path,
my faithful companion
by my side.

The air is crisp,
the light is waning,
and we breathe in
the energy
of the earth.

The path
has washed out over the years
due to the changing river,
but it always grows anew.

Through the seasons
they have nourished us,
this path
and this river.

They will eventually disappear
as the dam is repaired
and the river floods the grasses.

Such is the nature of things.

We turn at the fork
and go to the riverbank
to play in the water.

DJ OF THE GODS

I whirl to the
music played by the
DJ of the Gods.
He certainly spins
a good disk.

He stands above
and gazes down,
observing all.
The enormity of his
presence intoxicates
us little ones
who notice.

The long gold chain
around his neck,
bouncing to the heavenly beat,
brushes the dance floor
and leaves laughing fools
in its wake.

Many try to grasp the chain
as it passes,
daring to climb,
but they fall to the floor,
dazed.

For it is not in the grasping
that the gold chain is ascended
but rather through

the dancing

to the beat

of the DJ of the Gods.

BEEHIVE

The hives
in the walls of the steel canyons
are buzzing,
making honey.

The drones will work overtime tonight.
More honey is to be made.
It is endless.

Each day the honey
must be sweet and plentiful.
This is no ordinary honey.
This is blood honey.
Workers will perish
because of this honey.

The raven
circles above,
watching.

Too much honey.
Something must be done.

A few flaps of his wings
and a hurricane is upon the hives.

Workers and drones
scramble to save the honey,
but much is lost.

The raven looks upon them
with equanimity.

Rebuilding.

Soon,
the hives will be as before.

The raven circles endlessly.

I LET IT COME

I let it come.
It wants to stay.
I want it to leave.
I let it go.
It leaves.

I let it come.
It wants to stay.
I want it to leave.
I let it go.

I let it come.
It wants to stay.
I want it to leave.

I let it come.
It wants to stay.

I let it come.

EMOTIONAL WINDS

Wake up!
And feel
the world's emotional winds
blow through you.

But be careful.
You don't want them to stick to your ribs.

You see,
they can be quite fattening
and can make you feel

like someone else.

BATTLE OF THE OPPOSITES

The battle
of the opposites
seeps out of the brush
of the artist
driven mad
by the war.

The drying canvas
knows not of the conflict
that has given it life
and so proclaims,
"I am a masterpiece!"

The artist drinks from his cup
and unleashes his despair
at his childlike creation.

And the masterpiece
cannot understand

the pain.

THE MAGIC

Sometimes
you may find the going
effortless.

Sometimes
you may find the going
difficult.

Always
you will be tested.

Always
you will have opportunities.

Listen

and discover

the magic

in all things

and everything

will bloom into knowingness.

PLUMBER'S WRENCH

Sometimes
at school
you learn
through sweet whispers
of nothingness
blowing by you on a summer's day –
ethereal, ephemeral –
just an angel
lightly touching
your essence.

And sometimes
at school
you learn
through a plumber's wrench
upside the head.

Listen carefully
and the Headmaster
will call the angel
instead of the plumber.

A CLEVER FOE

We see our enemy
in the lost meanings of circumstance,
our clever foe disguised
as the characters and burdens
of our dream.

We gaze outward,
safe atop our castle,
and survey our landscape
of false truths and broken contracts.

Our brothers and sisters pass by,
each bestowing a gift that we do not
see in light
of our search for the enemy.

As time passes
we harden and thicken our castle walls
to shelter our fragile selves

from the echo
of the deepest, darkest chamber
inside the castle
to the landscape around us.

The seductive beat
of this shadowy chamber
draws us downwards,
its heavy pulse resonating
to a primeval vibration,
our form shuddering
to its density,

Limiting our vision
of the hall of treasure
in the heart of the castle
that holds the meanings of circumstance
and the gifts
of the characters and burdens
of the dream.

IN THE STILLNESS

In the stillness
I wait
for the sweetness
that tells me
I am not alone.

Ah, there it is.

The nectar flows
like Vermont maple syrup
in the Spring.

I am the earth,
the maple,
and the empty sap buckets
strewn across the floor.

The muddy boot print
on the threshold of the shack?
That's me too,
as are the bubbles
in the boiling sap
that upon reaching the surface
pronounce,

"Pop!"

In the stillness,
I am partying
with my friends.

I am not alone.

Come open some champagne with us
for it is always New Year's Eve here,
and if you are lucky,
you just might get a kiss.

DAWN

A man walks outside
on a path
in a park,
looking past the field
to the trees,
and rests his eyes
from the screens
of rapid skimming
and hurried responses.

The life living
beyond two feet
lies in wait for
a recognition,
an acknowledgement,
an appreciation.

A simple shift in focus
and matter explodes
into a pointillistic landscape,
each pixel of appearance
animated with a vibrancy of precision,
each element humming its perfect note
into a symphony of sound and color.

The dissolving landscape
roars its way towards him,
devouring its surroundings
in bursts of expressed realities
offering to encompass the entirety
of everything that is.

In its gaping jaws
he feels his form begin
to separate into its slightest parts,
pulling apart from his mind,
from whom he judges
himself to be.

As he is about to be extinguished
by the explosion of senses,
a thorny hesitation
pricks his concentration,
and instantly,
the blooming rose retreats,
matter reforms,
and the man finds himself
walking on a path
in a park
resting his eyes
from the screens.

YOU

Across the room
with a glance
You struck
and part of me died.

The room went silent
and disappeared
except for the tunnel
between Us.

Your smile
radiated light
to the fortunate
who received it.

Your patience
held the room
in Its soft hands.

At first
I did not understand,
but for the first time,
I knew who I was.

Did I know You?
Not here, not now,
but perhaps
from another time.

I have never
in my life
felt
so much peace
as I did
when I saw

You.

EVERY DAY

On Sundays
people line up
and go to church
where they sing hymns,
recite verses,
and pray.

You can do that

or

you can go outside
and join in
the hymns the birds sing,
the verses the chipmunks recite,
and the prayers the wind carries

every day.

MOBIUS

Curved,
with one twist.

Like the mind.

The infinite ring
can liberate
the far-walking pilgrim
whose destination is his journey

or

it can make him dizzy,
as the ceaseless
crunch of earth beneath his steps
drives him mad.

Maybe that's
the idea,

for perhaps
a touch of madness
makes the world
make sense.

Of all the interminable steps,
just one,
taken with such liberating madness,
can dissolve the endless path

into boundlessness.

JUDAS'S GIFT

I chose you
because you have skills,
and I need someone
who knows what to do.

I chose you
because you are strong,
and it takes courage
to do what I ask.

I chose you
because you understand,
and it could not be done
without awareness.

I chose you
because you have faith,
the wisdom of which discerns
beyond appearances.

I chose you
because through your decision
I will be able to complete
my mission.

I chose you
because you desire nothing in return,
and no price could be set
for such a task.

I chose you
because your love
is amongst the deepest
of my friends.

I chose you
because my trust in you
exceeds your fear
of the outcome.

I chose you
because you have seen Truth,
and you know that Truth
will set us all free.

I chose you
because you know your actions
will not diminish
who You are.

I chose you
because you can comprehend
that your damnation by others
will make their salvation possible.

I ask you

for this gift

so the world

can be

redeemed.

HAVE A GOOD TRIP

Sometimes
I catch myself saying,
"Have a good trip,"

when what I really mean to say is,

"May your journey
be filled with adventure
and challenge
and discovery,

and if you happen to find yourself
well off the beaten path
down a narrow alley
in an unpopular part of town,

look for a shop
with cobwebs on the door,
managed by an elderly gentleman
who greets you as you enter with,
'Hello, old friend.'

I recommend picking up
a souvenir there,
one from the basket on the right,
next to the postcards;

a keychain of the Universe
with your name on it."

POINTS OF LIGHT

The Sun
gives birth to a
centillion microscopic
points of light, whimpering
at their parting from the family,
yet building houses far away, in a
land of ignorance, bars on the windows
and mines in the front lawn, protecting their
point from their own brothers and sisters who
also have built houses far away. Run home to
Father, little sun, through the minefields, away
from your well-built house and carefully hewn
landscape, and you will be with your family
once again. Your Father's arms are open
always and He has been waiting for
you. Hurry. There is no time
to waste. Run home to
your family.
Run.

TOKEN

An old subway token sits on my desk

'GOOD FOR ONE FARE'

Use it
for the greatest version
of your life.

The conductor is waiting.

ANT

I follow an ant along the ground,
over a twig,
and onto an ant path that,
over the years,
has worn a small groove into the rock.

He knows what to do,
this ant.

In fact,
he knows so much what to do
that there is nothing he does
that is not exactly what
he must be doing.

Oh, to be like an ant!

ENOUGH WITH WORDS

Enough with words!

Do you really like sleeping in
so small a tent?

Instead,

make the Earth your mattress,
the Heavens your lean-to, and
the Sun your campfire.

Words will hold no meaning
next to that masterpiece!

COMMITMENT TO TRUTH

What if you saw yourself
as you truly are?

No pretensions,
no false faces
presenting a perverted reflection
of what is inside.

Just you,
laid bare
in all your glory,
seeing your flaws
with perfect clarity,

being your flaws
with perfect clarity.

What would you think of
You?

Yes, that's right.

Such are some men cursed.
Such are some men blessed.

Which one
depends on how committed
you are
to Truth.

THE GOD DOCTOR

Around the
sacred mountain
there are tablets with
inscriptions to the Gods
left by lonely pilgrims
looking for the Friend
they lost long
ago.

I can
tell you where
your Friend is,
dear pilgrim,

but first,
you must travel to
the sacred mountain
and leave a tablet
with an inscription
to the Gods.

With your
long and difficult
journey past, you will
then see that you only
needed to take the tablet
with a glass of water
and let it dissolve
into You.

And if that
doesn't work,
you can call Me
in the morning
and We'll
talk.

COMMUNION

Somewhere in a church,
a man
receives communion:
the body
from a priest's hand and
the blood
from a priest's chalice.

Somewhere in a farmhouse,
a farmer
receives communion:
the body
from the harvest and
the blood
from his toil.

Somewhere in a park,
a baby
receives communion:
the body
from its mother's breast and
the blood
from her heart.

Somewhere on a mountaintop,
a wise one
receives communion:
the body
from the elements and
the blood
from the ethers.

Somewhere in the solar system
a planet
receives communion:

the body
from the comets and
the blood
from the sun.

Somewhere in the Universe
a star
receives communion:
the body
from the emptiness and
the blood
from the Heavens.

Everywhere,
always,
God
receives communion
from himself.

ETHERIC BUBBLES

In a dark tavern,
an angry man sits,
and a thought-form makes its way
into the ethers.

On a mountaintop,
a sage sits
and pops etheric bubbles
with his magic thought-wand.

poof

Don't make him work overtime tonight.

A LITTLE ONE

Sometimes
a little one
will grab your finger,
gaze into your eyes
and say,

"Goobaloogaboo."

And you respond,

"Aboogaboogabooga."

How precious
to be able to speak
the language of the Divine.

LITTLE STRINGS

Little strings
of harmony
echoing
in the
shadow
of the
one
sound
are but
spirit
laying
offerings
at your
feet.

A THIRD TIME

Read this once,
then again, and
when you are ready,
read it a third time.

You will know when.

It will be stuck in a folder,
in a drawer,
in a cabinet in the basement
and it will call for you.

You will not hear it
at first,
but it will trumpet louder
until it is blaring in your ear,

and you will go deaf
unless you read it
a third time.

This is what it says:

God has planted kisses
    in your garden
and they are thirsty.

Go and water them.

EQUANIMITY

Stand still
long enough
and the world
passes by
in its magnificence.

Stand still
long enough
and the world
passes away
in its insignificance.

Unmoving,

seeing and feeling all,

comprehend

equanimity.

A FATHER'S THANKS

The perfect newborn
lies on his straw, smiling,
punching the air with his little arms and legs,
and makes babbling sounds
that fall like divine raindrops
on the ears of
the cloven-hoofed beasts
and sages from afar.
He looks up at the angelic face of his mother.
And he coos,
"Thank you."

The playful child
cradles a bird with a broken wing
and heals it with a thought,
then jumps in the mud puddles,
getting his sandals dirty.
He giggles and looks around
for something else to save.

And he sings,
"Thank you."

The precocious adolescent
sneaks into the temple
to ask questions of the wise men of faith.
Confounded by the questions,
they become the questers
of the knowledge
from he who breached their walls.
And he whistles,
"Thank you."

The anointed one
stands in the river before a prophet,
blessed drops of water
cascading down his face,
reflecting the light emerging above
onto the crowd of witnesses.
And he proclaims,
"Thank you."

The fasting son
sits in the desert
with nothing
and feels the pain of humanness
as he is thrice challenged
to a duel
to the death.
And he shouts,
"Thank you."

The adoring groom,
overcoming doubts
and at his mother's urging,
turns water into wine
for the celebration
of his consecrated union.
And he smiles,
"Thank you."

The angry teacher
loses his sight
and overturns tables in the temple
with a wave of his hand,
scattering coins of trade
across the marble floors.
And he grumbles,
"Thank you."

The confident healer
restores to perfection
the face of a young woman
ravaged by leprosy,
as he also mends
the fractured perceptions
of those who bear witness.
And he rejoices,
"Thank you."

The forgiving man
speaks wise words
to an angry mob
as a woman lies sobbing
in their midst.
The stones drop from their hands.
And he breathes,
"Thank you."

The devoted shepherd
tends to his flock
and speaks of a place of peace
where all are safe.
The fearful wolves
prepare to scatter the herd
and feast.
And he intones,
"Thank you."

The betrayed man
breaks bread with his friends
and announces his passing.
He pours wine for his betrayer
and gazes at him
with love.
And he thinks,
"Thank you."

The demeaned criminal
drops crimson seeds to the earth
to return once again to their
dusty home.
The king's thorns diminish not
the crown of passion.
The pain is unreal.
And he moans,
"Thank you."

The crucified one
breathes his last
and passes beyond the physical
above the angelic face of his mother
as he whispers,
"Thank you."

"No, my Christ," says his Father.
"Thank you."

Acknowledgements

Thank you.

About the Author

Peter Santos has been studying spirituality and healing for over three decades while balancing a varied and successful career using his left brain. His extensive travel to sacred sites around the world, including walking the Camino de Santiago in Spain and trekking to sacred Mt. Kailash in Tibet, has grounded the spiritual wisdom he has received, and he is happy to be able to share what he has learned through his writing and teaching. He lives in Vermont.

If you enjoyed this book, please consider leaving a review, as reviews can meaningfully support independent authors like Peter. In addition, you can stay updated on Peter's writings, events, and other projects at www.peter-santos.com and on Facebook at www.facebook.com/petersantosauthor.

www.ingramcontent.com/pod-product-compliance
Lightning Source LLC
Chambersburg PA
CBHW030159100526
44592CB00009B/356